W9-AXM-100

Copyright © 2018 by Puppy Dogs & Ice Cream, Inc.
All rights reserved. Published in the United States by Puppy Dogs & Ice Cream, Inc.
ISBN: 978-1-949474-19-0

For all inquiries, please contact us at:
info@puppysmiles.com

To see more of our books, visit us at:
www.PuppyDogsAndIceCream.com

TANTRUM

A CHILD IN THE WHITE HOUSE

WRITTEN BY
HILLARY EVANS

ILLUSTRATED BY
ANA NGUYEN

MAKE AMERICA GREAT AGAIN

I will be in Iowa all day and until Tuesday morning. Finally, after all these years of watching stupidity, we will MAKE AMERICA GREAT AGAIN!

4:38 AM - 30 JAN 2016

I'M THE PRESIDENT... DAMN IT!

FAKE NEWS

The Fake News Media is going CRAZY!
They are totally unhinged and in many ways,
after witnessing first hand the damage they do to so
many innocent and decent people, I enjoy watching.
In 7 years, when I am no longer in office,
their ratings will dry up and they will be gone!

6:34 AM - 31 JUL 2018

LIES!
ALL LIES!!
CNN
TRUMP: AMERICA'S DOWNFALL

FAMILY

The Democrats are forcing the breakup of families at the Border with their horrible and cruel legislative agenda. Any Immigration Bill MUST HAVE full funding for the Wall, end Catch & Release, Visa Lottery and Chain, and go to Merit Based Immigration. Go for it! WIN!

10:08 AM - 15 JUN 2018

WE WON'T LOSE HIM!

FRIENDS

Why would Kim Jong-un insult me by calling me "old," when I would NEVER call him "short and fat?" Oh well, I try so hard to be his friend - and maybe someday that will happen!

5:48 PM - 11 NOV 2017

DAY CARE
MY DICTATOR'S THE BIGGEST!

MILITARY

Space Force all the way!

9:03 AM - 9 AUG 2018

MY NAME IS TRUMP VADER!

ECONOMY

Our Economy is setting records on virtually every front -
Probably the best our country has ever done.
Tremendous value created since the Election.
The World is respecting us again!
Companies are moving back to the U.S.A.

3:04 AM - 24 AUG 2018

HOW DOES THIS TARIFF FEEL?

GLOBAL WARMING

In the East, it could be the COLDEST New Year's Eve on record. Perhaps we could use a little bit of that good old Global Warming that our Country, but not other countries, was going to pay TRILLIONS OF DOLLARS to protect against. Bundle up!

5:01 PM - 28 DEC 2017

Time OUT
LOOKS FINE TO ME... IT'S ONLY ONE DEGREE DIFFERENT.

IMMIGRATION/WALL

Mexico will pay for the wall - 100%!

9:58 PM - 31 AUG 2016

GET OUT
AND STAY OUT!

TWEETING

My use of social media is not Presidential -
it's MODERN DAY PRESIDENTIAL.
Make America Great Again!

3:41 PM - 1 JUL 2017

HE DID IT!!
Obama

POWER

North Korean Leader Kim Jong Un just stated that
the "Nuclear Button is on his desk at all times."
Will someone from his depleted and
food starved regime please inform him that
I too have a Nuclear Button, but it is
a much bigger & more powerful one than his,
and my Button works!

4:49 PM - 2 JAN 2018

MINE'S BIGGER!!
Show & tell

IN OFFICE

Time Magazine called to say that I was PROBABLY going to be named "Man (Person) of the Year," like last year, but I would have to agree to an interview and a major photo shoot. I said probably is no good and took a pass. Thanks anyway!

3:40 PM - 24 NOV 2017